El arte en acción

La pintura

Isabel Thomas

Heinemann Library
Chicago, Illinois

© 2006 Heinemann Library
a division of Reed Elsevier Inc.
Chicago, Illinois

Customer Service 888-454-2279

Visit our website at www.heinemannlibrary.com

All rights reserved. No part of this publication may be reproduced or transmitted in any form or by any means, electronic or mechanical, including photocopying, recording, taping, or any information storage and retrieval system, without permission in writing from the publisher.

Printed and bound in China by South China Printing Company Limited
Translation into Spanish produced by DoubleO Publishing Services
Photo research by Mica Brancic

09 08 07 06
10 9 8 7 6 5 4 3 2 1

Library of Congress Cataloging-in-Publication Data
Thomas, Isabel, 1980-   [Painting. Spanish]
  La pintura / Isabel Thomas.
      p. cm.   Translation of: Painting.
  Includes index.
  ISBN 1-4034-7410-9 (hc - library binding) -- ISBN 1-4034-7416-8 (pb)
  1. Painting--Technique--Juvenile literature.   I. Title.
  ND1146.T4818 2005
  751--dc22
                                                        2005026881

Acknowledgments
The author and publishers are grateful to the following for permission to reproduce copyright material: Corbis pp. 5, 19 (Ariel Skelley); Cumulus pp. 10, 13; GettyImages pp. 8, 14, 18 (Taxi); Harcourt Education pp. 6, 9, (Trevor Clifford); pp. 4, 7, 11, 12, 15, 16, 17, 20, 21, 22, 23, 24 (Tudor Photography)

Cover photograph of paint pots reproduced with permission of Getty (Photographers Choice)

Every effort has been made to contact copyright holders of any material reproduced in this book. Any omissions will be rectified in subsequent printings if notice is given to the publisher.

Many thanks to the teachers, library media specialists, reading instructors, and educational consultants who have helped develop the Read and Learn/Lee y aprende brand.

Algunas de las palabras aparecen en negrita, **como éstas**. Podrás encontrarlas en el glosario ilustrado en la página 23.

Contenido

¿Qué es el arte?. 4
¿Cuántos tipos de arte podemos hacer?. . . 6
¿Qué es la pintura?. 8
¿Qué tipos de pinturas puedo usar?. 10
¿Con qué puedo pintar?. 12
¿Qué puedo pintar?. 14
¿Qué más puedo pintar? 16
¿Qué me hace sentir la pintura? 18
¡Vamos a pintar!. 20
Prueba breve 22
Glosario ilustrado 23
Nota a padres y maestros. 24
Índice 24
Respuestas a la prueba breve 24

¿Qué es el arte?

El arte es algo que haces cuando eres **creativo**.

A la gente le gusta ver arte.

A la persona que hace arte se le llama artista.

¡Tú también puedes ser un artista!

¿Cuántos tipos de arte podemos hacer?

Podemos dibujar y pintar.

También podemos hacer collages e imágenes.

Las esculturas son otro tipo de arte.

El arte puede ser grande o pequeño.

¿Qué es la pintura?

Pintar es hacer una imagen con pinturas.

Los artistas pintan sobre papel especial o cartulina.

También puedes pintar algo que hayas hecho tú.

Estas niñas están pintando una escultura.

¿Qué tipos de pinturas puedo usar?

Algunas pinturas ya están listas para usar.

Las sacas apretando un tubo.

agua

pincel

pintura en polvo

Algunas pinturas tienen que mezclarse con agua.

Puedes hacer la pintura espesa o líquida.

¿Con qué puedo pintar?

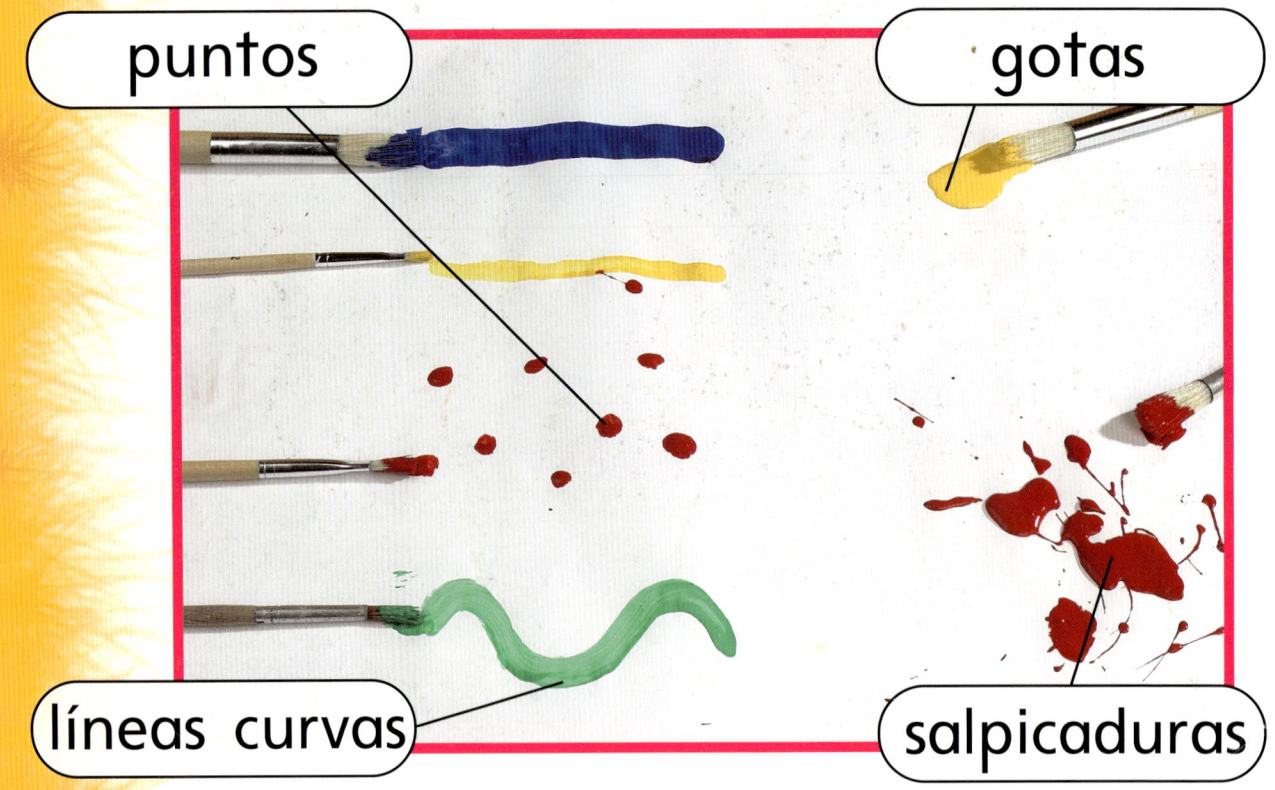

puntos

gotas

líneas curvas

salpicaduras

La mayoría de los artistas usan **pinceles** para pintar.

¡Fíjate en las marcas que puedes hacer con un pincel!

¡También puedes pintar con los dedos!

Las pinturas ensucian, así que ponte ropa vieja o un **delantal**.

¿Qué puedo pintar?

Puedes pintar imágenes de las cosas que ves.

Elige lugares u **objetos** que se vean interesantes.

Fíjate con cuidado en los colores y las formas.

Intenta copiarlos.

¿Qué más puedo pintar?

Pinta algo que te guste.

Piensa qué vas a poner en tu pintura.

Piensa en un día divertido, como un cumpleaños.

Intenta pintar lo que estás pensando.

¿Qué me hace sentir la pintura?

Pintar es divertido. Te sientes feliz cuando eres **creativo**.

Cuando muestras tus pinturas a tus amigos, te sientes orgulloso.

¡Vamos a pintar!

¡Vamos a pintar una mariposa!

1. Dobla una hoja de papel por la mitad y luego desdóblala.

2. Pinta el ala de una mariposa a un lado. Usa muchos colores y diseños.

3. Vuelve a doblar la hoja de papel por la mitad, mientras la pintura aún está fresca. Aprieta fuerte.

4. Desdobla la hoja y fíjate: ¡una mariposa **simétrica**!

Prueba breve

Todas estas cosas se usan para pintar.

¿Te acuerdas de cómo se llaman?

Busca las respuestas en la página 24.

Glosario ilustrado

delantal, página 13
una pieza que te pones para mantener tu ropa limpia

pincel, página 12
instrumento para poner pintura sobre papel. Un pincel tiene un mango y cerdas peludas.

creativo, página 4, 18
hacer algo usando tus propias ideas y cómo te sientes por dentro

objeto, página 14
cosa que ves o tocas

simétrico, página 21
cuando algo tiene dos lados iguales

Nota a padres y maestros

Leer para informarse es parte importante del desarrollo de la lectura en el niño. El aprendizaje comienza con una pregunta sobre algo. Ayuden a los niños a pensar que son investigadores y anímenlos a hacer preguntas sobre el mundo que los rodea. Cada capítulo en este libro comienza con una pregunta. Lean juntos la pregunta. Fíjense en las imágenes. Hablen sobre cuál piensan que puede ser la respuesta. Después lean el texto para averiguar si sus predicciones fueron correctas. Piensen en otras preguntas que podrían hacer sobre el tema y comenten dónde podrían buscar las respuestas. Ayuden a los niños a utilizar el glosario ilustrado y el índice para practicar un nuevo vocabulario y destrezas de investigación.

Índice

collage 6
colores y formas 15
delantal 13
esculturas 7, 9
imágenes 6
lugares y objetos 14
papel y cartulina 8
pinceles 12, 22
pintar con los dedos 13
pintura de mariposa 20 y 21
pinturas 10 y 11, 22

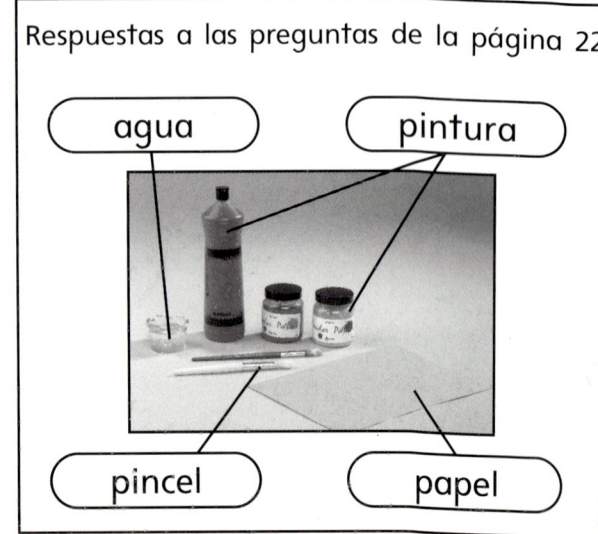

Respuestas a las preguntas de la página 22

ANIMAL EXPLORERS

CARNIVORES

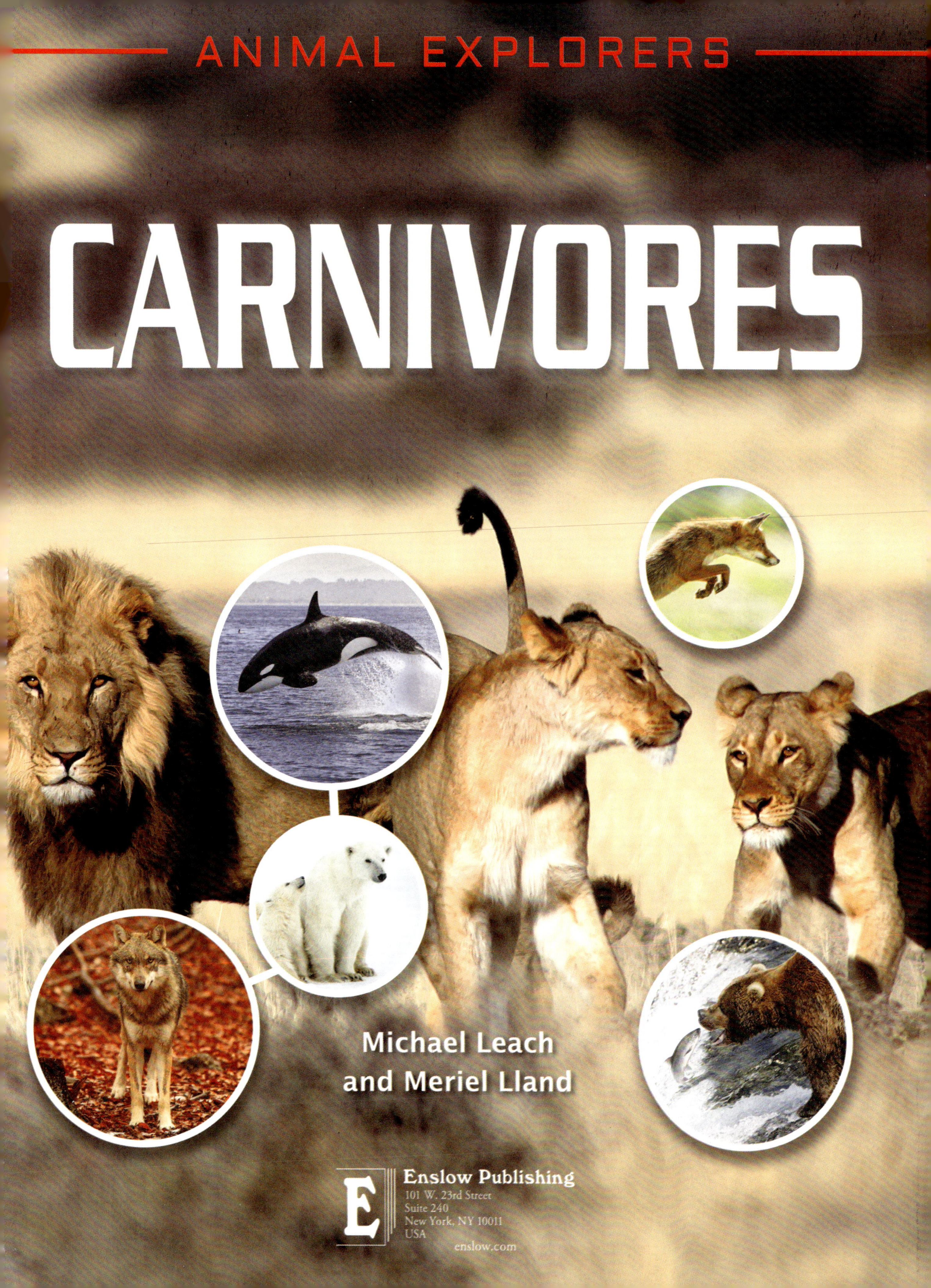

Michael Leach
and Meriel Lland

Enslow Publishing
101 W. 23rd Street
Suite 240
New York, NY 10011
USA
enslow.com

This edition published in 2020 by Enslow Publishing, LLC
101 W. 23rd Street, Suite 240, New York, NY 10011

Copyright © Arcturus Holdings Ltd 2020

All rights reserved.

No part of this book may be reproduced by any means without the written permission of the publisher.

Cataloging-in-Publication Data

Names: Leach, Michael. | Lland, Meriel.
Title: Carnivores / Michael Leach and Meriel Lland.
Description: New York : Enslow Publishing, 2020. | Series: Animal explorers | Includes bibliographical references and index.
Identifiers: ISBN 9781978509832 (library bound) | ISBN 9781978509818 (pbk.) | ISBN 9781978509825 (6 pack)
Subjects: LCSH: Carnivora—Juvenile literature. | Carnivorous animals—Juvenile literature.
Classification: LCC QL737.C2 L43 2020 | DDC 599.7—dc23

Printed in the United States of America

To Our Readers: We have done our best to make sure all website addresses in this book were active and appropriate when we went to press. However, the author and the publisher have no control over and assume no liability for the material available on those websites or on any websites they may link to. Any comments or suggestions can be sent by email to customerservice@enslow.com.

Photo Credits:
Every attempt has been made to clear copyright. Should there be any inadvertent omission, please apply to the publisher for rectification.

Key: b-bottom, t-top, c-center, l-left, r-right

Alamy: 4–5 (Ian Cruickshank), 9cr (Fernando Quevedo de Oliveira), 22bl (Michael DeYoung/Design Pics Inc), 23br (Animals by Vision); FLPA: 6–7 (Frans Lanting), 12–13 (Karl Van Ginderdeuren), 13bl (Juan-Carlos Munoz), 16–17 (Norbert Wu), 18–19 (Christopher Swan/Biosphoto), 20cr (Photo Researchers), 20cl & 32br (Christian Ziegler), 22–23 (Michael Durham; Shutterstock: cover and title page; 4cl (Puwadol Jaturawutthichai), 4br (Alen thien), 5tr (Giedrilius), 5cl (David Bokuchava), 5br (Dennis van de Water), 6–7 (LMIMAGES), 6bl (belizar), 7tl (Medvedeva Oxana), 7br (Luna Photogood), 8bl (Victor Lapaev), 9br (Spreadthesign), 10–11 (Warren Metcalf), 10bl (Michal Ninger), 11cr (davemhuntphotography), 11br (SaveJungle), 12br (Spreadthesign), 13cr & 31bl (hansenexposed), 14–15 (Sergey Uryadnikov), 14cl (sirtravelalot), 15tr (elmm), 15br (Photo by Lola), 16cl, 17cr (vladsilver), 17br (Maquiladora), 18cl (Michael Smith/ITWP), 18br (Kurilin Gennadiy Nikolaevich), 19b & 31br (Tory Kallman), 20–21 (Worraket), 21tr (Mush322), 23tr (SaveJungle), 24–25 (Vladimir Wrangel), 24b (Antero Topp), 25tr (Val_Iva), 25br (Jana Horova) 26tr (Mark Bridger), 26tl (Vaclav Sebek), 26cr (belizar), 26bl (Marek Velechovsky), 26br (Molly NZ), 27tl (Aleksey Stemmer), 27tr (Seb c'est bien), 27cl (MISS KANITHAR AIUMLA-OR), 27br (Kris Clifford), 27bl (maradon 333), 28cl (Dmitri Gomon), 29tr (FloridaStock), 29bl (markusmayer).

CONTENTS

Introduction 4
Carnivores 6
Cats 8
Wolves 10
Foxes 12
Bears 14
The Seal Family 16
Whales and Dolphins 18
Bats 20
Otters 22
Mongooses 24
Fun Facts 26
Your Questions Answered 28
Glossary 30
Further Information 31
Index 32

Introduction

An animal is a living organism made up of cells. It feeds, senses, and responds to its surroundings, moves, and reproduces. Scientists have identified nearly nine million species of living animals, but there are many more to be found.

Life Appears

Single-celled life forms appeared around four billion years ago. Sponges—the first animals—appeared a billion years ago. Over time, more complicated animals evolved and some also became extinct. Dinosaurs were the dominant land animals for 165 million years before they died out 65 million years ago.

Fossilized skull of the dinosaur *Tyrannosaurus rex*

Rhinoceros hornbills are birds that live in Southeast Asian rain forests. Birds are warm-blooded animals with backbones. They have wings and most can fly.

Leaf beetle, an insect

Classifying Life

Scientists organize living things into groups with shared characteristics. The two main kinds of animal are ones with backbones (vertebrates) and ones without (invertebrates). Arthropods make up the biggest invertebrate group. They have segmented bodies and jointed limbs. Insects, spiders, and crabs are all arthropods.

Warm- and Cold-Blooded

Most animals are ectothermic, or "cold-blooded." Their body temperature is controlled by their environment. Mammals and birds are endothermic, or "warm-blooded." Their bodies can generate their own heat, so they can survive in much colder habitats.

Musk ox, a mammal

Langurs in a city

Fragile Earth

We are lucky to share our world with an extraordinary richness of animals. It is important to protect our wildlife. When humans pollute or damage the environment, we harm both animals and people. The future is in our hands.

Animal Habitats

The place where an animal lives is called its habitat. Animals have evolved to inhabit just about every environment on Earth, from tropical rain forests and coral reefs to deserts, mountaintops, and ice floes. They even survive in cities.

Giant leaf-tailed gecko, vulnerable because of habitat loss

5

Carnivores

Carnivores are animals that eat other animals. There are nearly 300 mammal species that are true carnivores, although some are omnivores, meaning they eat both animals and plants. Mammals are warm-blooded, breathe air, and have a backbone. They give birth to live young, which they feed with milk from the mother. They live all over the globe and in all habitats.

Carnivore Features

Carnivorous mammals are built to spot, chase, and kill prey. They have forward-facing eyes that judge distance and long legs for speed. Their large brains help them to hunt strategically. Some carnivores live solitary lives, but others live in packs or groups and hunt as a team.

Carnivores have specialized teeth: long, pointed canines at the front of the mouth for killing and sharp-edged carnassials at the back for slicing through meat.

Living Fast

Meat is rich in energy, so carnivores don't need to feed often. When they do hunt, it helps to be in peak condition. Any illness or slight injury slows them down. Predators' lives are dangerous and can be short. More predators die of starvation than old age.

A leopard can eat 9 pounds (4 kg) of meat at a time. It only needs to hunt twice a week, and can spend the rest of the time resting.

The hyena's crushing bite lets it reach the rich marrow inside bones. Around half of its diet is carrion.

SPOTTED HYENA
CROCUTA CROCUTA

Habitat: Woodlands, grasslands, scrub; sub-Saharan Africa
Length: Male 4.3 feet (1.3 m); female 4.6 feet (1.4 m)
Weight: Male 121 pounds (55 kg); female 132 pounds (60 kg)
Diet: Mammals
Life span: Up to 20 years
Wild population: 40,000; Least Concern

7

Cats

Cats are carnivores with soft fur, a short snout, and sharp claws. The first cats appeared around 30 million years ago. Today wild cats live everywhere except Australia and the Antarctic. There are 41 wild cat species. Four—the lion, tiger, jaguar, and leopard—are in their own family: the big cats.

Forward-facing eyes let this Bengal tiger judge distance accurately. Most cats are nocturnal hunters and see well in the dark.

Getting a Grip

Cats use their sharp claws to grab prey. In most species the claws retract into the paw when they are not being used. However, the cheetah's claws are always out. They grip the ground and stop the cat slipping when it runs.

The cheetah is the world's fastest mammal. In short bursts it can run at 65 miles (105 km) per hour.

Hearing is a tiger's most important sense. The cat can swivel each ear independently to pick up faraway sounds from all directions.

Long, sensitive whiskers can detect small air movements. This is useful for finding prey at night.

Stripes camouflage tigers in forests and grasslands. Tigers spend an hour every day licking their fur. This removes loose hairs and keeps the coat clean and warm.

The large, sharp canine teeth kill prey. Behind these, the carnassial teeth are used for cutting through flesh.

Family Life

Lions are the only cats that hunt and live in groups. All other species are loners that come together only to breed. Most cats live in forests or grasslands, but some have adapted to other environments. Sand cats live in deserts, hunting birds and lizards and surviving on very little water.

Lions live in family groups called prides. A typical pride includes related lionesses, their cubs, and a couple of adult males.

BENGAL TIGER
PANTHERA TIGRIS
"CAT TIGER"

Habitat: Forests, swamps, grasslands; South Asia
Length: Male 9.8 feet (3 m); female 8.5 feet (2.6 m)
Weight: Male 551 pounds (250 kg); female 353 pounds (160 kg)
Diet: Mammals—e.g. deer, wild pigs
Life span: Up to 18 years
Wild population: 2,000–2,500; Endangered

9

Wolves

Flattened ears give this wolf's body a streamlined shape when it runs. In an encounter with another wolf, flattened ears would be a sign of submission.

The largest members of the dog family, timber wolves were once the most widely distributed predator on Earth. Today they live only in remote areas of North America and Eurasia, far from humans, but their population is stable. However, the red wolf from the eastern United States and the Ethiopian wolf are both endangered.

Falling Numbers

For centuries, humans hunted wolves because they feared attacks on themselves and their livestock. They also cleared wolves' forest habitats for farmland. Today the timber wolf is extinct in much of Western Europe, Mexico, and the United States.

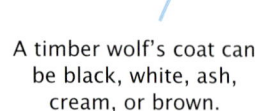

A timber wolf's coat can be black, white, ash, cream, or brown.

Wolves can smell prey up to 1 mile (1.6 km) away. The nose also tells them whether another wolf is a friend or rival, and whether it has just eaten.

The thick coat is waterproof and warm, thanks to a dense undercoat. Wolves survive at temperatures down to −40°F (−40°C).

10

Tails are used for balance and communication. Dominant wolves hold their tail high. Low-ranking animals curl their tail between their legs.

Long legs and stamina mean a wolf can cover 60 miles (96 km) in just six hours. During a chase it can reach 35 miles (56 km) per hour.

Wolves mark territory by howling and leaving strong-smelling droppings.

Family Affair

A pack's territory can range from just 11.6 square miles (30 sq km) to as much as 770 square miles (2,000 sq km). A typical pack contains about a dozen animals. Only the dominant male and female breed. The other pack members work together to protect the cubs.

TIMBER WOLF
CANIS LUPUS
"WOLF DOG"

Habitat: Forests, tundra, mountains, grasslands; North America, Asia, Europe
Length: 9.8 feet (3 m)
Weight: Male 99 pounds (45 kg); female 85 pounds (38.5 kg)
Diet: Mammals—e.g. deer, bison
Life span: Up to 12 years
Wild population: Unknown; Least Concern

Foxes

Foxes are the smallest members of the dog family. They have triangular faces, pointed ears, and bushy tails. Intelligent and adaptable, foxes live everywhere except the Antarctic. They have a range of calls, barks, and yelps to communicate fear, warnings, threats, and playfulness.

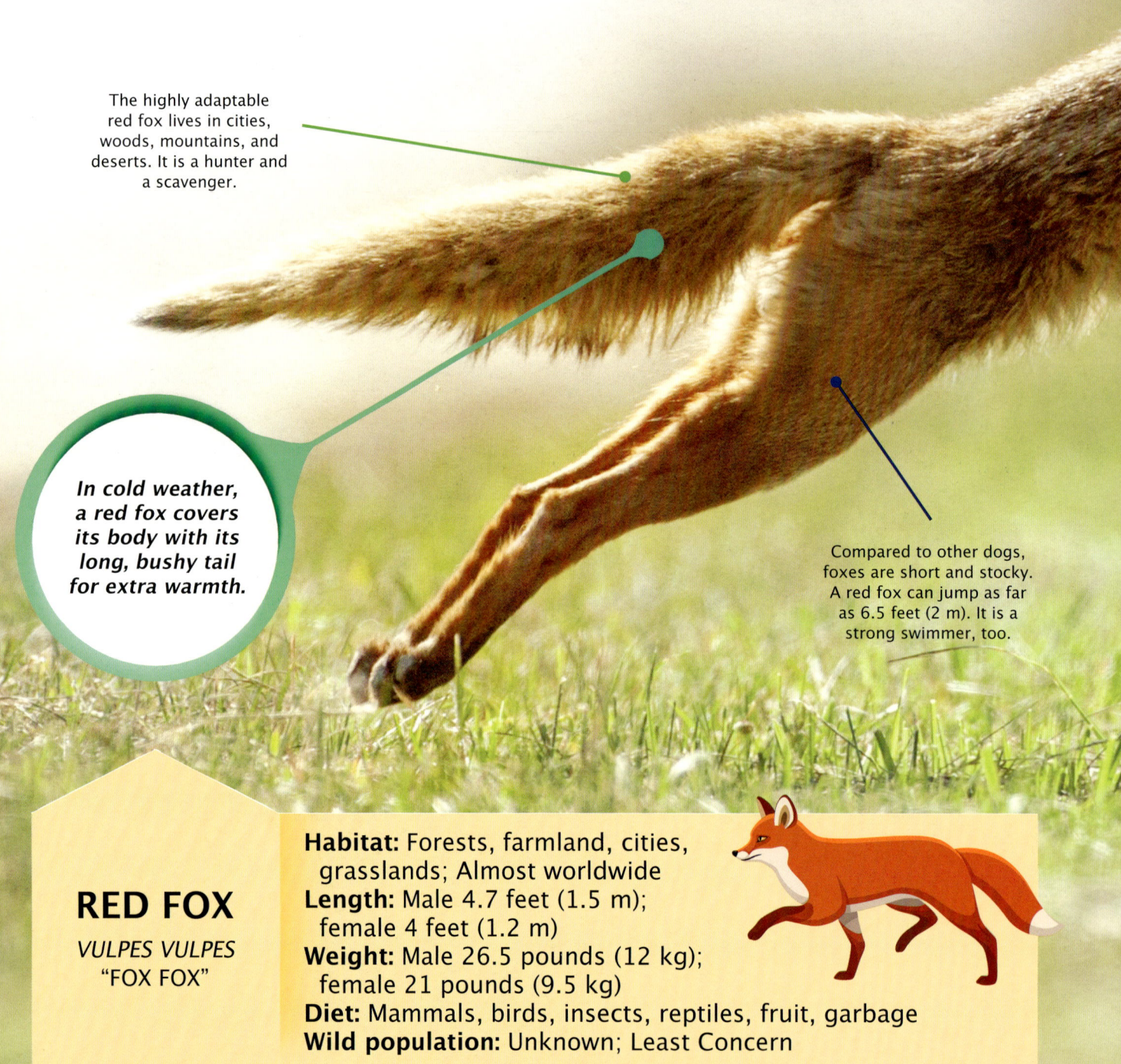

The highly adaptable red fox lives in cities, woods, mountains, and deserts. It is a hunter and a scavenger.

In cold weather, a red fox covers its body with its long, bushy tail for extra warmth.

Compared to other dogs, foxes are short and stocky. A red fox can jump as far as 6.5 feet (2 m). It is a strong swimmer, too.

RED FOX
VULPES VULPES
"FOX FOX"

Habitat: Forests, farmland, cities, grasslands; Almost worldwide
Length: Male 4.7 feet (1.5 m); female 4 feet (1.2 m)
Weight: Male 26.5 pounds (12 kg); female 21 pounds (9.5 kg)
Diet: Mammals, birds, insects, reptiles, fruit, garbage
Wild population: Unknown; Least Concern

The red fox uses its senses of hearing and smell to pinpoint the position of prey animals.

Unlike most dogs, a fox cannot bare its teeth.

Skilled Survivor

The 12 "true foxes" include red foxes, Arctic foxes, and kit foxes. The red fox is the most widespread carnivore. It eats anything, from invertebrates and small mammals to grasses and kitchen waste. Foxes bury stashes of food in times of plenty and then return to them when they are hungry.

The Arctic fox has adapted to live in the cold north. Its winter coat is white to blend in with the snow.

Desert Dweller

The smallest wild dog is the fennec fox, which lives in the driest parts of North Africa. It stays cool by losing excess body heat through its huge ears. The ears also funnel sounds so that the fox can locate prey at night and underground. Prey provides most of the fox's moisture.

The fennec fox is the smallest wild dog. Standing only 8 inches (20 cm) tall, it is about the same size as a pet kitten.

Bears

There are eight species of bear. They live in Asia, Europe, and the Americas. Most are omnivores that feed on plants and insects and live in forest habitats. They only eat meat if they find carrion or a slow-moving, weak animal. Polar bears are the exception. These speedy hunters are carnivores.

The Bear's Year

Polar bears are active all year round, but other bears in the far north—grizzlies and black bears—hibernate in winter. In warmer places, there is plenty of food all year. Species such as Indian sloth bears don't need a winter sleep.

Underneath the dense, waterproof fur is a thick layer of fatty blubber to protect the polar bear from the cold.

When salmon swim upriver to breed in late summer, grizzlies have a fishy feast! It helps them put on weight ready for hibernation.

Bears are usually loners, but mothers look after their cubs for two years or more. The cubs grow quickly because their mother's milk is about one-third fat.

POLAR BEAR
URSUS MARITIMUS
"SEA BEAR"

Habitat: Tundra, ice floes, oceans; Arctic
Length: Male 9.2 feet (2.8 m); female 7.2 feet (2.4 m)
Weight: Male 1,323 pounds (600 kg); female 573 pounds (260 kg)
Diet: Seals, carrion, fish
Life span: Up to 25 years
Wild population: 30,000; Vulnerable

All bears have amazingly sensitive noses. They can smell food up to 30 miles (50 km) away.

Picky Pandas

Most bears eat many kinds of food, but pandas are choosy. Ninety-nine percent of their diet is bamboo. Pandas live in the mountains of China. They are threatened by habitat loss and only around 1,500 are left in the wild.

The bear's pale, creamy coat helps to camouflage it against the snow.

Most mammals are digitigrade—they walk on their toes. Bears (and humans) are plantigrade—they stand on the soles of their feet.

Pandas spend most of their waking hours eating. They eat about 600 bamboo stems a day.

The Seal Family

The zoological name for seals and their relatives is pinnipeds, which means "fin-foot." Their webbed back feet provide the power for swimming, while the front legs are used for walking—clumsily!—on land. Seals, sea lions, and walruses all live in cool water and avoid tropical seas.

In Their Element

Underwater, seals pursue prey at speeds up to 17 miles (27 km) per hour, thanks to their streamlined bodies. However, like all marine mammals, they must surface to breathe. Elephant seals hold their breath longest—their dives last 100 minutes or more.

Large eyes can see well in the low light levels underwater.

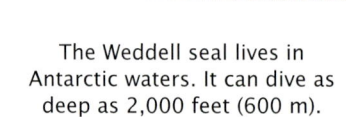

The common seal is a true or earless seal. It does not have external ear flaps.

The Weddell seal lives in Antarctic waters. It can dive as deep as 2,000 feet (600 m).

The nostrils completely close when the seal is diving. The animal has a good sense of smell on land.

Whiskers sense tiny movements in the water, helping the seal locate prey when it is too dark to see.

A thick layer of blubber beneath the skin insulates the seal (keeps it warm) and aids buoyancy.

Pinnipeds in Danger

The pinnipeds are made up of three families: true or earless seals, eared seals (sea lions and fur seals), and walruses. Almost a third are at risk, threatened mainly by climate change and pollution. In the past, many fur seals were hunted close to extinction for their fur.

In the past, walruses have been hunted for their ivory tusks. Today, the trade in ivory is illegal.

COMMON SEAL

PHOCA VITULINA
"CALF-LIKE SEAL"

Habitat: North Sea, Baltic, North Atlantic, North Pacific
Length: Male 5.9 feet (1.8 m); female 5.2 feet (1.6 m)
Weight: Male 265 pounds (120 kg); female 198 pounds (90 kg)
Diet: Seals, carrion, fish
Life span: Up to 20 years
Wild population: 350,000; Least Concern

Whales and Dolphins

A pod of short-beaked common dolphins work together to attack a bait ball of blue jack mackerel.

Dolphins and whales are cetaceans—highly intelligent mammals that mate, feed, and give birth in all the world's oceans. Cetaceans are split into two groups: baleen whales, which eat invertebrates, and toothed whales, such as dolphins, which take much bigger prey.

Filter Feeders

Blue whales, humpbacks, and other baleen whales are filter feeders. These huge animals have sieve-like plates inside their mouths to filter plankton, krill, or other foods from the water.

This is a baby humpback whale. Baby whales drink the equivalent of one-and-a-third bathtubs full of mother's milk a day!

COMMON DOLPHIN
DELPHINUS DELPHIS
"DOLPHIN DOLPHIN"

Habitat: Atlantic, Pacific, Indian Ocean, Mediterranean Sea
Length: Male 7.2 feet (2.2 m); female 6.9 feet (2.1 m)
Weight: Male 265 pounds (120 kg); female 231 pounds (105 kg)
Diet: Fish, squid, octopus
Life span: Around 20 years
Wild population: Unknown; Least Concern

Dolphins travel in pods of up to 1,000. They live mainly in warm waters, hunting fish and squid.

The dolphins herded the fish into a ball shape. It is easy to pick off individuals from the edge of the ball.

Finding Food

Dolphins and other toothed whales use echolocation to navigate and find prey. They produce clicks that travel through the water and then bounce back to them off objects. Cetaceans also use noises to communicate with each other. Humpbacks are known for their long, complex songs.

The orca is the largest species of dolphin. It mostly hunts seals, but also eats squid, seabirds, fish, and even turtles.

Bats

There are around 1,100 living species of bats, making up about one-fifth of all mammal species. They live worldwide apart from in the frozen Arctic and Antarctic. Bats are the only mammals that have evolved true powered flight. Other "flying" mammals, such as the flying squirrel, can only glide.

Batty Diets

Seventy percent of bats feed on insects. One brown bat ate 1,000 mosquitoes in an hour! Bats have adapted to hunt other sources of meat, such as birds, frogs, lizards, fish, or other bats. Vampire bats are famous for drinking blood from cows, horses, or sheep. The largest bats, called megabats or flying foxes, feed on fruit.

The spectral vampire bat is the world's largest carnivorous bat. It feeds on small birds and reptiles.

The greater bulldog bat is a fishing bat. It uses its feet to snatch fish or insects from lakes or rivers.

Bat Senses

Bats have keen eyesight and a good sense of smell. However, most bats find food using echolocation. They send out high-frequency sound waves, then listen to how the waves bounce back off objects. From this, the bats can work out an object's exact position, size, and shape.

By hanging upside down, bats can drop into the air and then fly. It takes less energy than taking off upward like a bird.

LYLE'S FLYING FOX
PTEROPUS LYLEI

Habitat: Forests, farmland, cities; Southeast Asia
Length: 8.7 inches (22 cm)
Wingspan: 35.4 inches (90 cm)
Weight: 0.9 pounds (390 g)
Diet: Ripe fruit, nectar
Life span: Up to 20 years
Wild population: Unknown; Decreasing

Unlike most other bats, flying foxes do not eat insects nor do they have echolocation. They use eyesight and smell to find flowers and fruit to eat.

The wings are thin skin stretched over thin bones. Sleeping bats wrap their wings around themselves for warmth.

21

Otters

The 13 otter species are members of the mustelid family, along with badgers, wolverines, and weasels. These predators are found everywhere except Australia and the Antarctic. Otters have slim, streamlined bodies, short legs, webbed feet, and a strong tail.

Clever with Clams

Sea otters are one of the few mammals that use tools. When feeding on shellfish, a sea otter swims on its back and balances a flat stone on its chest. Grasping the prey in its front paws, it smashes open the shell on the rock.

The Eurasian otter lives in fresh water and along coasts.

The otter makes many different calls and whistles to communicate.

Sea otters can weigh up to 99 pounds (45 kg). A very thick coat of fur keeps them warm in their ocean home.

EURASIAN OTTER

LUTRA LUTRA
"OTTER OTTER"

Habitat: Lakes, rivers, coasts; Europe, Asia
Length: Male 4.3 feet (1.3 m); female 3.6 feet (1.1 m)
Weight: Male 22 pounds (10 kg); female 15.4 pounds (7 kg)
Diet: Fish, amphibians, crustaceans
Life span: Up to 10 years
Wild population: Unknown; Near Threatened

The otter's head is flat, with the nose and eyes high on the skull. When it swims, only the very top of the head is visible.

Otter Basics

For otters, the main diet is fish, but they will eat almost any small animal. Apart from the sea otters, all species hunt both in water and on land, in daylight or darkness. Most are very territorial and mark their home range with piles of smelly droppings called spraint.

Long, sensitive whiskers can find food by touch.

The longest mustelid is the endangered giant otter, which lives in South America. It can be up to 5.6 feet (1.7 m) long.

23

Mongooses

Mongooses are native to Africa and India. Although they look like weasels, mongooses are more closely related to cats. Most mongooses are omnivores—their main food is meat, but they also eat plants, insects, and eggs.

Excellent senses and fast reflexes make meerkats very successful hunters.

Meerkats mostly eat insects, but they also hunt scorpions, lizards, snakes, and small birds.

Meerkats are mongooses adapted to survive in the dry habitats of southern Africa. They live in family groups of up to 30 animals.

Social or Solitary?

Most mongoose species are solitary animals. Others, including meerkats, yellow mongooses, and banded mongooses, live in social groups called colonies. Living together lets them share different jobs, such as building burrows, hunting for food, bringing up kits, and keeping a look out for predators.

This banded mongoose is acting as sentinel. If it spots an eagle, jackal, or other predator, it will warn the rest of the colony.

24

MEERKAT
SURICATA SURICATTA

Habitat: Deserts; Southern Africa
Length: Male 20 inches (50 cm); female 17.7 inches (45 cm)
Weight: Male 26.5 ounces (750 g); female 25.4 ounces (720 g)
Diet: Insects, arachnids, reptiles, small birds
Life span: Up to 12 years
Wild population: Unknown; Least Concern

Meerkats and other mongooses have long, sharp claws for digging. They build underground burrows where they sleep and give birth.

Natural Born Killers

Mongooses have been introduced to islands around the world to control overpopulations of rats and mice. However, mongooses are such good hunters that they have killed local wildlife as well as the pests. It is now illegal to introduce them into new countries.

This yellow mongoose has been fortunate enough to kill a small bird. Its usual diet is insects, spiders, and scorpions.

The legs are short enough to move in underground burrows, but fast enough to run at a top speed of 30 miles (48 km) per hour.

25

Fun Facts

Now that you have discovered lots about different kinds of mammals, boost your knowledge further with these 10 quick facts!

Spotted hyenas live in enormous clans of up to 80 animals. They are sometimes called "laughing hyenas" because of their whooping call.

The largest cat on record was a Siberian tiger that weighed 845 pounds (384 kg)—about the same as 90 pet cats!

The maned wolf of South America is a member of the dog family, but it is not a true wolf. Most of its diet is made up of fruit and vegetation.

Most foxes have 42 teeth, but the bat-eared fox has 48. Its teeth are extremely pointy and help it crunch up termites and other small animals.

The smallest bear is the sun bear. It grows no bigger than a ten-year-old child, but its tongue is an amazing 10 inches (25 cm) long!

The Saimaa ringed seal is the rarest pinniped. It is found in only one lake in Finland, and the total population is just 320.

Blue whales are the largest animals that have ever lived on Earth. Adults can be 89 feet (27 m) long and weigh more than 160 tons (143 tonnes).

The world's biggest bat is the giant golden-crowned flying fox from the Philippines. It weighs 2.6 pounds (1.2 kg) and has a 5.6-foot (1.7 m) wingspan.

Sea otters sleep in groups, called rafts, of up to 100 animals. They hold paws and wrap strands of seaweed around their bodies so they don't drift away.

Snake venom does not affect mongooses. An 11-pound (5 kg) mongoose would not even notice a cobra bite that would kill a human!

27

Your Questions Answered

We know an incredible amount about the creatures that populate our planet—from the deepest oceans to the highest mountains. But there is always more to discover. Scientists are continuing to find out incredible details about the relationship between predator and prey and many other aspects of a carnivore's life and behavior. Here are some questions about meat-eating mammals that can help you discover more about these fascinating creatures.

Conservation programs have helped protect the Amur leopard and allowed its numbers to increase.

Which cat species is the most endangered?

Today, many animals in the wild are threatened. This can have a lot of reasons—from climate change and habitat loss to disease and hunting. Whatever the cause, it most likely stems from human activity. This is no different for endangered cat species, some of which are only present in very tiny numbers. The most threatened is the Amur leopard, which lives in Russia and China. There may only be about 100 animals alive in the wild today. However, the good news is that their numbers have increased over the past few years; at one point, they were down to a mere 30.

How closely are pet dogs related to wolves?

Dogs were first domesticated (kept as pets) thousands, maybe even hundreds of thousands of years ago. They have been companions to humans ever since. For the longest time, scientists believed that today's pet dog evolved from the gray wolf, but recent studies have shown that instead, both have evolved from a common wolf-like ancestor who died out about 10,000 years ago. While dogs and wolves can breed with each other, and have many similar physical and behavioral features, domestic dogs have evolved through a very close relationship to humans, which means there are also many traits that set them apart from their wild cousins.

Why are polar bears endangered?

The habitat of polar bears is one of the most fragile regions on Earth—the Arctic is heavily affected by climate change, which has an immediate impact on polar bears. The Arctic goes through a cycle throughout the year, whereby parts of the ocean freeze over in winter, to then gradually melt and form ice floes in the summer. Polar bears rely on this sea ice; they use it as a hunting platform, a breeding ground, and a resting place. However, climate change has meant that, in recent years, the ice has been melting more quickly and for longer periods, "pushing" the bears on land or forcing them to swim for very long stretches to reach new floes.

Climate change is severely endangering the polar bear's habitat.

Are all mustelids good swimmers?

Mustelids are a group of mammals who all have similar physical features—thick fur, clawed feet, and anal scent glands. They are short, active hunters, who live in most parts of the world (apart from many smaller islands, Australia, Antarctica, and the Arctic). They have varied habitats, and are divided into "terrestrial" and "aquatic" mustelids. Although that doesn't mean they can or can't swim—all mustelids are agile hunters, and even those who don't normally seek out water can swim if necessary.

Why are mongooses immune to snake venom?

There are many animals that have developed ways of protecting themselves against venom. Apart from thick fur or other physical features, these creatures often have antivenin, a substance that neutralizes the effects of venom, in their blood. In mongooses, it's not antivenin in the blood that protects them from a cobra bite, but a mutation on each of their body cells that blocks the venom from causing any damage.

Mongooses have an unusual way of protecting themselves against cobra venom.

Glossary

blubber A thick layer of insulating fat under the skin of some mammals that live in cold environments.

buoyancy The ability or tendency to float on water.

camouflage To blend in with one's surroundings.

cetacean A marine or freshwater mammal with paddle-shaped forelimbs, no back limbs, and a flattened tail.

climate change A long-term change in Earth's climate, especially a rise in average temperatures.

echolocation A method of finding food or other objects by detecting reflected sounds.

excess An amount that is more than necessary.

extinct Describes an animal that has died out forever.

fortunate Lucky.

hibernate To slow the body down in winter to a kind of sleep.

high-frequency In sound waves, those that occur very often in a short space of time. High-frequency sound waves produce a very high-pitched sound.

insulate To protect against heat or cold.

marrow A soft, fatty substance stored in the core of bones.

mustelid A mammal in the weasel family with a long body, short legs, and musky scent glands under the tail.

omnivore An animal that eats plants and meat.

prey An animal that is hunted and eaten by other animals for food.

scavenger An animal that feeds on dead creatures.

strategically Done with careful planning.

streamlined Shaped in a way that provides very little resistance to airflow or water flow.

submission Behavior displayed when yielding to a stronger force.

venom A chemical that is injected into another animal to paralyze or kill.

Further Information

BOOKS

Broom, Jenny, and Katie Scott. *Animalium*. Somerville, MA: Big Picture Press, 2014.

Davies, Nicola, and Lorna Scobie. *The Variety of Life*. London, UK: Hodder Children's Books, 2017.

Dipper, Frances, and Alice Pattullo. *Pocket Guide to Whales, Dolphins and Other Marine Mammals*. London, UK: Lincoln Children's Books, 2018.

Higgins, Nadia. *Deadly Adorable Animals*. Minneapolis, MN: Lerner Publications, 2013.

Spelman, Lucy. *Animal Encyclopedia: 2,500 Animals with Photos, Maps, and More!* Washington, DC: National Geographic Kids, 2012.

WEBSITES

DK Find Out!: Carnivores
www.dkfindout.com/us/animals-and-nature/food-chains/carnivores
Read all about carnivores on this page.

Ducksters: Mammals
www.ducksters.com/animals/mammals.php
Head to this website to find out all there is to know about mammals.

Index

B
badger 22
bait ball 18
baleen 18
bat 20–21, 27
bat, vampire 20
bear 14–15, 26, 29
bear, grizzly 14
bear, panda 15
bear, polar 14, 15, 29
blubber 14, 17

C
camouflage 9, 15
carrion 7, 14, 15, 17
cetacean 18–19
cheetah 8
claw 8, 25, 29
colony 24
communication 11, 12, 19, 22

D
dog 10, 11, 12, 13, 26, 28
dolphin 18, 19

E
echolocation 19, 20, 21

F
filter feeder 18
fish 14, 15, 17, 18, 19, 20, 22, 23
flying fox 20, 21, 27
fox 12–13, 26
fox, Arctic 13
fox, fennec 13
fox, red 12, 13
fur 8, 9, 14, 17, 22, 29

H
hibernate 14
hunt 6, 7, 8, 9, 10, 12, 14, 17, 19, 20, 23, 24, 25, 28, 29
hyena 6, 7, 26

I
invertebrate 4, 13, 18

J
jaguar 8

K
krill 18

L
leopard 7, 8, 28
lion 8, 9

M
mammal 5, 6, 7, 8, 9, 11, 12, 13, 15, 16, 18, 20, 22, 26, 28, 29
marine 16
meerkat 24, 25
mongoose 24–25, 27, 29
mustelid 22, 23, 29

O
omnivore 14, 24
orca 19
otter 22–23, 27
otter, Eurasian 22, 23
otter, sea 22, 23, 27

P
pack 6, 11
plankton 18

pod 18, 19
predator 7, 10, 22, 24, 28
prey 6, 8, 9, 10, 13, 16, 18, 19, 22, 28
pride 9

S
sea lion 16, 17
seal, common 16, 17
seal, Weddell 16

T
teeth 6, 9, 13, 26
territory 11, 23
tiger 8, 9, 26

W
walrus 16, 17
warm-blooded 4, 5, 6
whale 18, 19, 27
whiskers 9, 16, 23
wolf 10–11, 26, 28
wolf, timber 10, 11

32

Children's 599.7 LEA
Leach, Michael
Carnivores

08/30/21